GEOGRAPHY *for fun*

Maps and Plans

Pam Robson

Franklin Watts
London • Sydney

This edition published in 2003
© Aladdin Books Ltd 2001

Produced by
Aladdin Books Ltd
28 Percy Street
London W1T 2BZ

*First published in Great Britain
in 2001 by*
Franklin Watts
96 Leonard Street
London EC2A 4XD

ISBN 0-7496-5351-5

Editor: Kathy Gemmell

Designer: Simon Morse

Illustrator: Tony Kenyon

All photographs provided by
Select Pictures, except page 28,
provided by NASA.

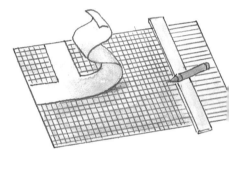

A CIP catalogue record for this book
is available from the British Library.

The author, Pam Robson, is an experienced teacher.
She has written and advised on many books for children
on geography and science subjects.

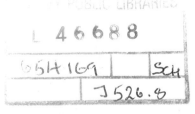

CONTENTS

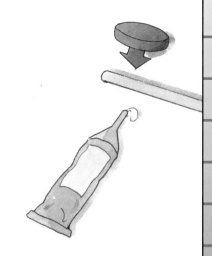

INTRODUCTION

Geography is about people and places and all the changes that take place in the world. How the shape of the land changes over time. How people use landmarks to find their way from place to place. How people alter landscapes when they build roads and houses and chop down forests. Geography is about all these things. To help you find out about the world, you need to know where places are and how to find them on plans and maps.

1 Look out for numbers like this. Each step for the projects inside the book has been numbered in this way. To draw the maps and make the models shown in each project, make sure that you follow the steps in the right order.

MORE IDEAS
● Look out for the More Ideas boxes. These either contain further information about the project on the page or suggest other interesting things for you to make or do.
● Remember, geography is all around you – you can use the More Ideas boxes to help you think up your own geography projects.

HELPFUL HINTS

● Look out for the Helpful Hints — they give you tips for some of the projects.

● Look at the Glossary at the back of this book to find out what important words mean.

● Always use the most up-to-date maps and atlases.

● Use the atlas index to find the location of the place you are looking for.

WARNING

● This sign means that you must take extra care when doing the project. Always tell an adult where you are going and what you are doing.

● Be especially careful when you are out collecting information. Try to take measurements with someone else, then you can both check that you don't bump into anything when taking notes!

LEFT AND RIGHT

Drivers on busy roads read route maps or follow signposts to find whether to turn left or right on a journey. Hikers use compasses and maps to find their way. All travellers look for landmarks, such as a particular tree, hill or building, to help them recognise where they are. Inside mazes there are many turnings, but no landmarks or signposts to point the way.

AMAZING MAZE

Make this maze game and help the elephant and giraffe take all the correct turns to reach the water hole.

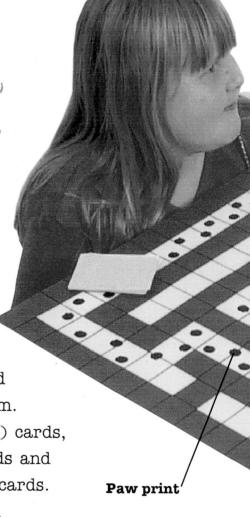

Paw print

1 Copy the African grassland maze in the photograph onto a squared board. Draw the pathways first, then decorate them with paw prints.

x 8

x 6

x 6

2 Cut out twenty pieces of stiff card measuring 8 cm by 5 cm. Design six 'turn left' (L) cards, six 'turn right' (R) cards and eight 'go forwards' (F) cards. Decorate the cards with different animals.

3 Make an animal counter for each player by drawing a picture onto a circle of stiff card and glueing it onto a bottle top. If you have toy animals, you could use them instead. Place the counters at the entrance to the maze.

4 The aim of the game is to reach the water hole first. Stack the cards face down. Take it in turns to pick a card. Turn your counter in the direction of the arrow on the card. If you pick a 'go forwards' card, you can move to the next junction, but only if you are facing the right way. If you can't move, miss your go. Replace the cards at the bottom of the pile.

MORE IDEAS

● Play again – in reverse. This time, begin at the water hole. The first one to reach the entrance to the maze is the winner.

● Practise giving directions. Ask a friend to find their way from your school to your home, or from one classroom to another. Write down when to turn left or right and whether there are any landmarks to look out for.

NORTH OR SOUTH?

A long time ago, ships had to sail in sight of land to know where they were. Sailors found their way using landmarks. Then it was discovered that magnetic stones called lodestones pointed towards north when suspended. These were the first compasses. Sailors were then able to sail away from coasts to discover new lands. The first maps had compass roses pointing towards the Orient (the east), which was believed to be the centre of the world.

COMPASS ROSE

Finding the way with a compass and map is now called orienteering. To do any orienteering, you need to know the points on the compass. Make a compass rose to help you remember them.

1 Use a ruler to draw a four-point compass rose. This shows the four main directions: north (N), east (E), south (S) and west (W). Label these clockwise from the top. Use a protractor to draw more accurately: the clockwise turn between each point is a right angle of 90 degrees.

2 To make an eight-point compass rose, rule lines halfway between each of the four main points. Mark these directions NE, SE, SW, NW. Colour your compass rose. On early maps, north is shown by a fleur-de-lys design like the one shown here. The clockwise turn between each of the eight points is half of a right angle, which is 45 degrees.

HELPFUL HINTS

● Think of a saying to help you remember the clockwise order of north, east, south and west, such as 'Nine, Eight, Seven, Wait'.

● Find north by pointing the hour hand of a watch towards the Sun. (Make sure the watch is telling the right time!) Lay the head of a matchstick halfway between the hour hand and twelve, as shown below. The match head will now be pointing south and the other end will be pointing north.

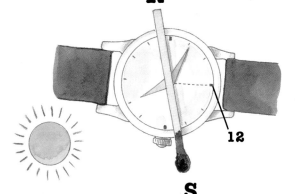

TAKING BEARINGS

● You can work out the exact position of a landmark by measuring where it is in relation to a fixed position. This is called taking a bearing. Bearings are worked out by measuring angles clockwise from north.

N
90°
E

● Choose a landmark that you can see from your garden or school, and work out its bearing. First find north. You can do this using a watch (see left), or by lining up north on a map with north on an orienteering compass. Now measure the clockwise turn from north to the direction of the landmark. This is its bearing.

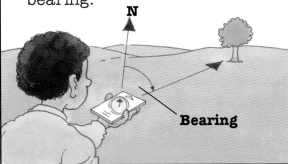

Bearing

BIRD'S-EYE VIEW

Objects look different when viewed from above.

A bird in the sky sees everything below in 2D (two dimensions) because objects on the ground look flat. Birds cannot see how high objects are. Someone standing on the ground sees the same objects in 3D (three dimensions). They *can* see how high the objects are. A plan of an object or place is always drawn in 2D. A plan is a bird's-eye view.

3D TO 2D

To make a yellow bus drive along this 2D street plan, you will need two button magnets, a length of dowelling, a large sheet of white card, a small sheet of yellow card, coloured paper, scissors and glue.

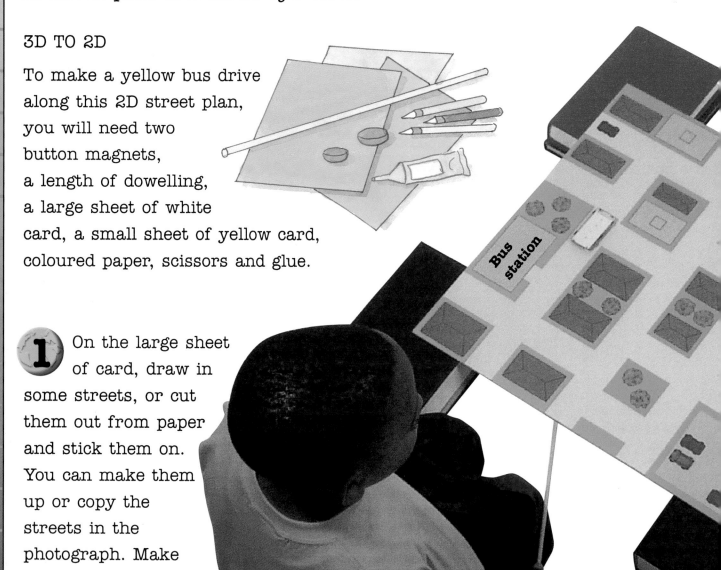

Bus station

1 On the large sheet of card, draw in some streets, or cut them out from paper and stick them on. You can make them up or copy the streets in the photograph. Make sure you leave spaces to put in buildings.

2 The 2D shapes, or symbols, drawn in the left column of the key below show what objects look like from above. Each 2D shape represents a 3D object, like a house, a car or a tree. Draw and colour the 2D shapes onto your plan.

 = **House**

 =  **Car**

 = **Block of flats**

 = **Tree**

3 Support the plan on some thick books to leave a space beneath. Now draw and cut out a 2D bus from yellow card. Make sure it is the right size to fit your street plan. Glue a button magnet to the bottom of the bus.

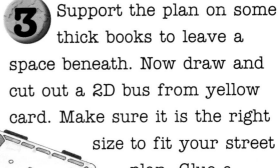

4 Glue another magnet to the dowelling to make a stick magnet. Place the bus on the plan. Move the stick magnet underneath the plan to make the bus go.

5 Now write a story describing how the bus gets from one place to another on your plan. Put in landmarks and say where the bus turns.

School

The bus drives out of the bus station and turns left. It drives past the trees on the left, and turns right into Meadow Road. At the block of flats, it turns left into the High Street then right into School Lane. It stops outside the school.

MORE IDEAS
● Make sure your street plan has a compass rose marked on it. Now write directions for the route of the yellow bus using N, E, S and W instead of left and right.

BIGGER AND SMALLER

Bees are much smaller than elephants. But a picture of a bee can look larger than it really is, while a picture of an elephant can look smaller than it really is. In the same way, a plan or map of a place looks much smaller than the real place. Drawing something smaller or bigger than it really is, but keeping it exactly the same shape, is called drawing to scale.

1 Choose a large picture of a famous landmark from a magazine. Glue the picture onto a sheet of paper and draw a grid of large squares over it.

SHRINK THAT PICTURE

To draw a picture to scale, you need squared paper. To reduce the size, use paper with smaller squares but keep the number of squares the same.

2 On squared paper with small squares, count and cut out the same number of squares that you drew on the large grid. Glue your small grid onto card. Now copy the shape of the picture carefully, square by square, onto the smaller grid.

The famous landmark in this picture is the Taj Mahal in India.

MORE IDEAS

Draw a scale plan of a playground or park close to where you live. You can measure distances by taking paces (steps), so you don't need a tape measure. Tell an adult what you are planning.

● You will need a pencil and some paper.

First find out which way is north (see page 9). Then pace out the size of the area. Write down how many paces you take in each direction. Note where the entrances and exits are. Sketch the position of objects, such as litter bins and seats.

● Use centimetre squared paper to draw out your plan. One pace on the ground can stand for 1 cm on your plan. This means that your scale is 1 cm = 1 pace. Write this on your plan. Draw a compass rose. Use 2D symbols to show the position of objects in the playground.

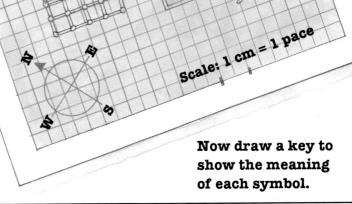

Playground

N E S W

Scale: 1 cm = 1 pace

Now draw a key to show the meaning of each symbol.

PLANS AND SYMBOLS

A plan or map needs to be large-scale in order to show important details like footpaths and houses. Large-scale means that lots of detail but only a small area can be shown. Most countries have large-scale maps showing different parts of the country. In Britain, these are called Ordnance Survey (OS) maps. Street plans are larger scale than OS maps – they even show the names of roads and buildings on them. Buildings often act as landmarks.

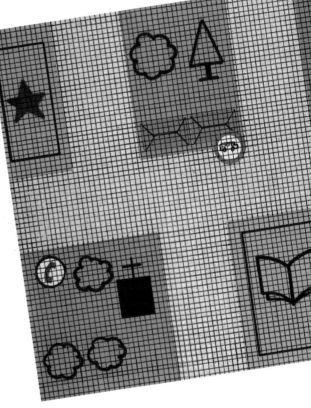

LARGE-SCALE STREET PLAN

Make a large-scale street plan to show the position of the different buildings in a street near your house or school.

1 Ask permission from an adult to carry out a street survey. Always work with a friend and watch out for traffic. Pace out distances between buildings and write down the measurements. Note down the position of each building and what it is used for. Find north (see page 9).

2 Use the measurements to draw a street plan onto centimetre squared paper. Use a scale of 1 cm equals one pace. Draw a compass rose.

3 Design 2D symbols for the different buildings and draw them onto your plan. Draw a key for the symbols.

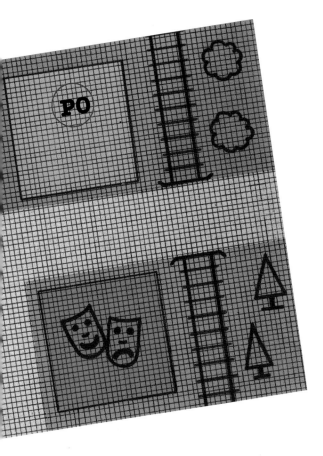

KEY TO PLAN
Keys explain the meaning of colours and symbols used on maps and plans. The key below explains the symbols used on the street plan.

★ Police station

✝ Church

📖 Library

(PO) Post Office

✉ Private house

🚌 Bus stop

Bridge

🎭 Theatre / Cinema

📞 Public telephone

🛤 Railway

🌲 Coniferous tree

☁ Broad-leaved tree

HELPFUL HINTS
● Some symbols are international and are understood worldwide. Look at the key box above or the key on an OS map of a town or city for ideas for symbols. Or you can make up your own.

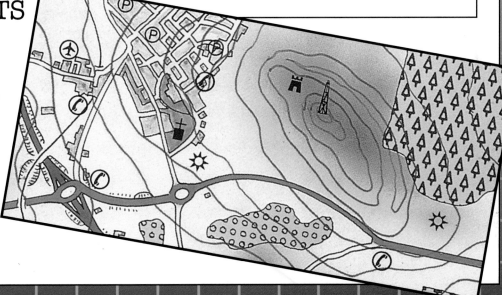

READING STREET PLANS

Street plans show the 2D shapes and positions of different buildings and objects, but they cannot show the height of buildings. There are many different kinds of home. Some people live in flats, which are in high buildings. Others live in houses. A 3D model of a street can show the height of all the buildings.

HIGH HOPES

From your street plan, you can construct a 3D model of a real place. Use paper, card and clean junk materials or natural materials like twigs and pebbles.

1 First, you need more information about the buildings on your street plan. Take photographs or make drawings of them. Count the number of floors in blocks of flats.

2 Make your model larger scale than your street plan. Draw a grid onto card with larger squares than your plan, but make sure it has exactly the same number of squares. Cut out strips of paper for streets and glue them in the correct position.

3 Draw a 2D pattern on card for each building, as shown. Make sure you know how wide and deep each building is (count the squares it covers on the plan). Score, fold and glue the pattern. Fold more card for a sloping roof. Draw or stick on doors and windows. Place the buildings on the model.

(1) **Width**
(2) **Depth**
(3) **Number of floors**

4 Shape some conifer trees from cones of green paper, as shown. Make broad-leaved trees from crumpled tissue paper. Make tree trunks from twigs. Glue the trunks onto card bases or push them into plasticine. Position your trees on the model.

MORE IDEAS
● Add smaller objects to your model, like litter bins and telephone boxes. Make signposts and traffic lights.
● Does the road have a pedestrian crossing? You could add plasticine people walking around.

HELPFUL HINTS
● Make features like bridges from coloured paper and cardboard.
● Finish off buildings by painting them. Do any painting before placing the buildings on the model.
● Make sure any entrances face the right way.

COLOURS AND CONTOURS

Small-scale maps cover a wider area than large-scale ones, but do not show as much detail. The shape of large areas of land can be shown on small-scale relief maps. Different colours are often used to show the height of the land. On large-scale OS maps, the height of the land is shown by brown lines called contours. Contours are lines joining places that are the same height above sea level.

SINK A MOUNTAIN

Contour lines show the height of the land in 2D. Make a 2D contour map by taking measurements from a sinking plasticine mountain.

1 You will need some plasticine, a straight-sided plastic bowl, a jug of water, a ruler and a cocktail stick.

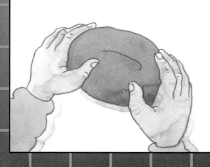

2 Shape a mountain from plasticine and put it inside the bowl. Place a centimetre ruler upright against the side of the bowl.

3 Pour in 2 cm of water. Use the cocktail stick to mark a line around the mountain at the water level. Pour in another 2 cm and mark a line at the new water level. Repeat until the water reaches the summit (top) of the mountain.

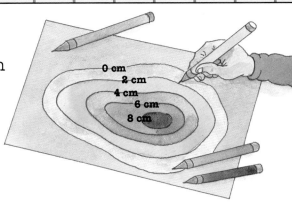

0 cm
2 cm
4 cm
6 cm
8 cm

4 Lift the mountain out of the bowl. Look at it from above and observe the pattern of the lines. Draw a contour map, like the one above, of what you see. Write the correct measurements on the contour lines. Colour the spaces between the contours in different shades.

RELIEF MAPS

● Look for small-scale relief maps in an atlas. Some relief maps look like 3D pictures. Hill shading is used so that hills and mountains – like the Dolomites, Apennines and Alps shown on this map of Italy – look like real hills and mountains. Different colours often show height above sea level. Sometimes hachuring (cross marking) is used to show the shape of high ground.

Dolomites

Alps

Po Valley

Apennines

ITALY

SICILY

FIXING POSITION

Describing the position of an object on a page, when there are many objects scattered at random, is tricky. A grid laid over the page makes it much easier. The exact position of every object can then be given using a grid reference, which is the column name followed by the row number.

BIRTHDAY PUZZLE

Send a coded birthday message using a grid. To decode the message, you have to decode the grid references listed in the correct order.

1 Fold a sheet of card in half. Cut a grid of 8 x 11 squares from 2 cm squared paper. Glue it to the front of the card. Cut the card to size if necessary. Leave spaces, as shown, to write in the column names and row numbers.

Leave space for column names along the bottom.

Leave space for row numbers up the left-hand side.

2 Now write each of the letters of the alphabet in a square on the grid. Jumble the letters so you do not read them in order. Draw party objects in the empty squares.

3 From left to right along the bottom of the grid, fill in the column names A to G. Up the left-hand side of the grid, fill in the row numbers 1 to 10. Leave the bottom left square blank.

4 Inside the card, write grid references for each of the letters of the message you want to write. Make sure you write them in the correct order. Use the grid to work out the message below.

A5	B9	A10	A10	B6
E10	F8	C8	F6	A5	A7	B9	B6
B9	D3	B4	E1

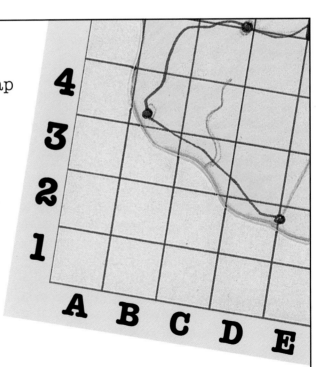

GRID MAPS

● In an atlas, a grid map with numbered spaces can cover a whole country. Each square has a grid reference. This makes it easy to locate a particular place on the map, such as a town or city. On this map, there is a town in square B4.

FINDING THE WAY

A routefinder map, such as an Ordnance Survey map, is larger scale than a country map. It covers an area of 100 square km, divided into 1 km squares by a numbered grid. The numbered lines are called eastings and northings. A reference with four figures in it refers to the southwest (SW) corner of a particular square on the map.

FINDING THE WAY

Hikers use routefinder maps because they show paths and landmarks. Can you find the church on this routefinder?

1 The 4-figure grid reference for the church is 03, 06. The easting is 03 and the northing is 06. Count along to 03, then count up to 06, and you are at the SW corner of the square with the church in it.

2 There are three bridges marked on the map. Can you find them? One bridge is in square 02, 05. Another bridge is in square 07, 08. Remember that the easting always comes first, followed by the northing.

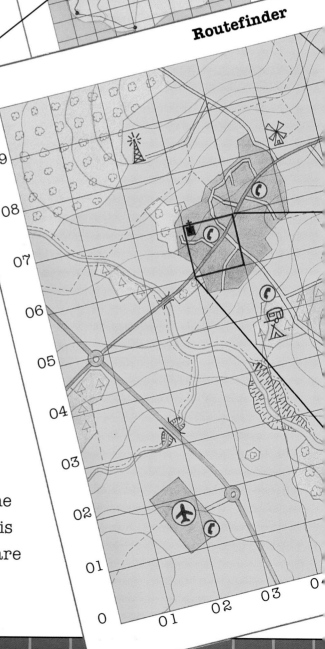

Country map

Routefinder

3 Imagine a magnifying glass placed over square 03, 06. Now imagine that square divided up again by a grid of 100 smaller squares. This lets you see much more detail on that section of the map. It is now a street plan. You can now give a 6-figure grid reference, which describes the exact position of a landmark inside the 100 squares on the grid.

MORE IDEAS

● Can you think what kind of map a cyclist needs? Like a hiker, who needs to know where the best footpaths are, a cyclist needs to locate good cycle routes.

● Look at the street plan. Which feature is next to the police station, at grid reference 034, 066?

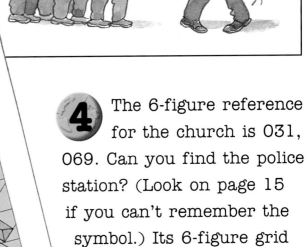

Street plan

4 The 6-figure reference for the church is 031, 069. Can you find the police station? (Look on page 15 if you can't remember the symbol.) Its 6-figure grid reference is 035, 066.

PICTURE MAPS

Maps are designed differently to highlight particular features of a place. Relief maps show the shape of the land. Political maps show countries, their capital cities and their borders. Thematic maps tell us interesting facts about different countries. They give information about weather and climate, farming and wildlife. Maps like this need a key. Picture maps can tell a story without a key because pictures are used instead of symbols.

PICTURE THIS

Make a picture map of your favourite place. It may be a town, a city or a country that you have visited on holiday.

1 If you have chosen a country, copy its shape from an atlas. For a city, draw a map of the region. Draw and colour pictures of the things you like about the place you have chosen. You can also stick on photographs or pictures from magazines.

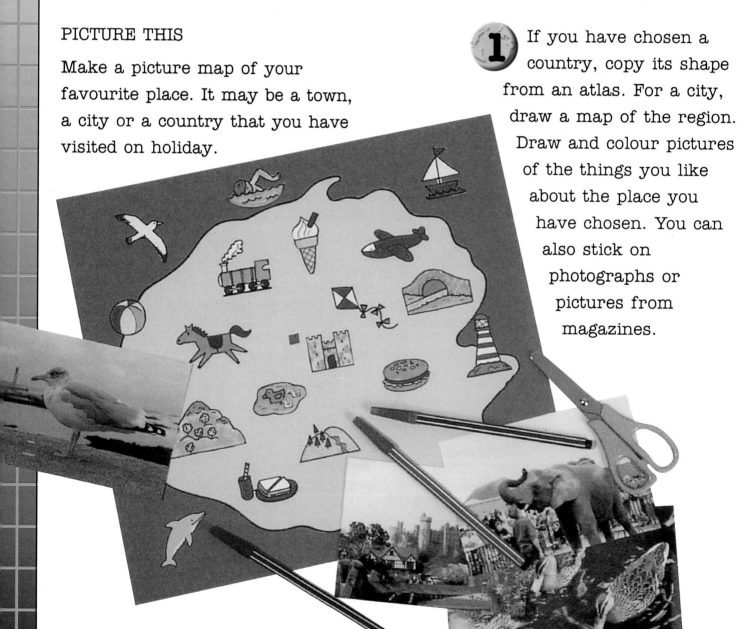

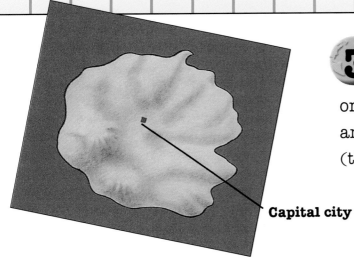

Capital city

3 Political maps of districts use colours to show different counties or regions. Was your holiday place in an urban area (a town) or a rural area (the countryside)?

2 Try to find a relief map of your favourite place in an atlas. Do you remember whether it is flat or mountainous? A relief map like this one shows the shape of the land as a 3D picture. Other relief maps have contours showing height above sea level.

WEATHER MAPS
● Weather maps use symbols that can be understood anywhere in the world because they are like pictures.
● Look at weather maps on TV. What kind of weather did you have on holiday? Was it sunny or rainy?
● Make weather pictures for your holiday map. What kind of climate does your holiday place usually have?

25

4 One kind of thematic picture map is a farming map, which shows where food is grown. Foods that come from your holiday place might be sold in supermarkets on the other side of the world.

COUNTRIES AND CONTINENTS

The world is divided into seven large landmasses called continents. Each country of the world is part of a continent. USA is a country in the continent of North America. Egypt is a country in the continent of Africa. France is a country in the continent of Europe.

COUNTRY MAP

To make this collage map of the country of Italy, you will need an atlas, a sheet of card, coloured paper, glue, scissors, coloured pencils, plasticine and some cocktail sticks.

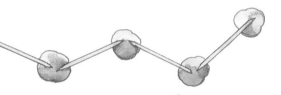

1 Find Italy in an atlas. Look closely at its shape. Do you think it looks like a boot? Copy or trace the shape of Italy onto the sheet of card. Colour it in, then use plasticine to fix cocktail sticks around the edge for your coastline. Snap the cocktail sticks to get the right shape.

2 Copy Italy's flag and stick it onto your map. Show the position of Rome, the capital city. Now stick on pictures of things you know about Italy. Look at other kinds of map to help you. You can even stick on some dried pasta!

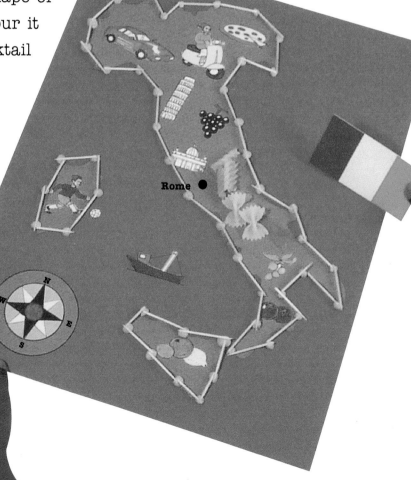

Rome ●

CONTINENT PUZZLE

The seven continents
are North America,
South America,
Oceania, Africa, Asia, Europe
and Antarctica. On this page are
the outlines of six of them,
each in a different colour.
They are not in their correct
positions. Can you
find the shape of
each one and
arrange them
correctly?

On many
world maps,
including the
projection
shown below,
Antarctica is
not shown
(see pages
28-30).

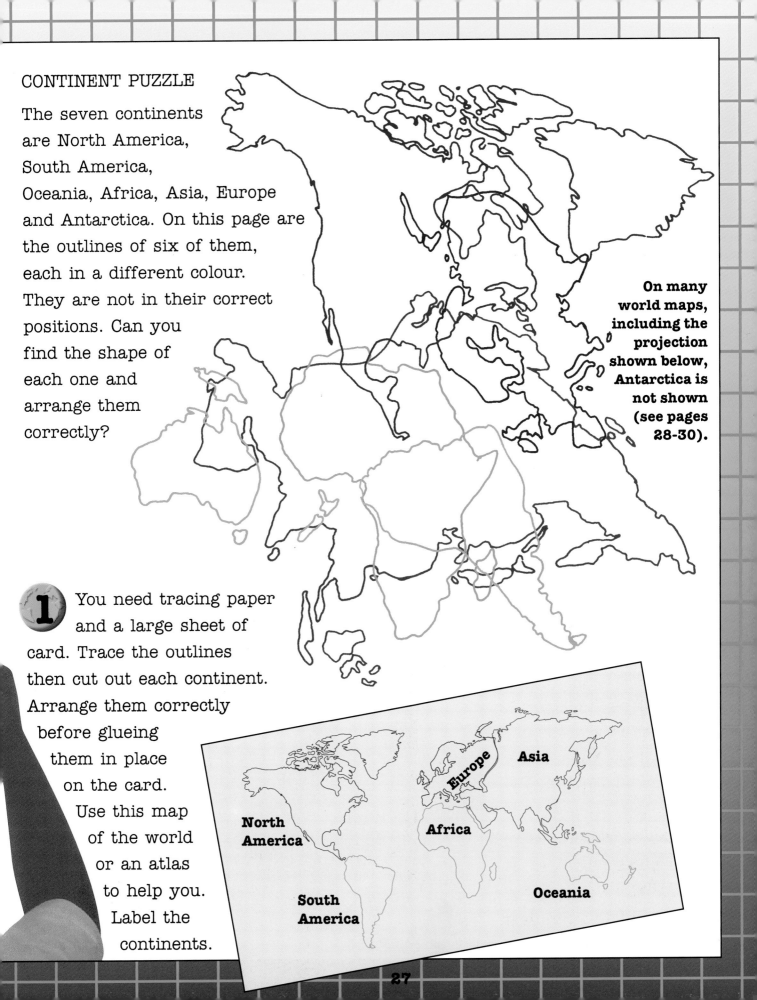

1 You need tracing paper
and a large sheet of
card. Trace the outlines
then cut out each continent.
Arrange them correctly
before glueing
them in place
on the card.
Use this map
of the world
or an atlas
to help you.
Label the
continents.

North
America

South
America

Europe

Africa

Asia

Oceania

GLOBES AND MAPS

When viewed from space, the Earth is like a 3D spheroid (globe). A flat map of the whole Earth is 2D. The true shapes of all countries and continents cannot be shown on a flat map. A globe is covered by a grid which cartographers (map-makers) use to turn the shape of the Earth into a flat map.

ORANGE PEEL WORLD

If you peel an orange, keeping the peel whole, it is impossible to lay the peel flat. Changing a globe to a map is like that. But you can make a globe from a specially shaped map that allows for the Earth's curves.

1 First trace this map of the world. Colour the land green and the seas blue.

2 Fold your 2D flat map at the fold marks to make a 3D globe shape. Then join the poles together and attach with sticky tape.

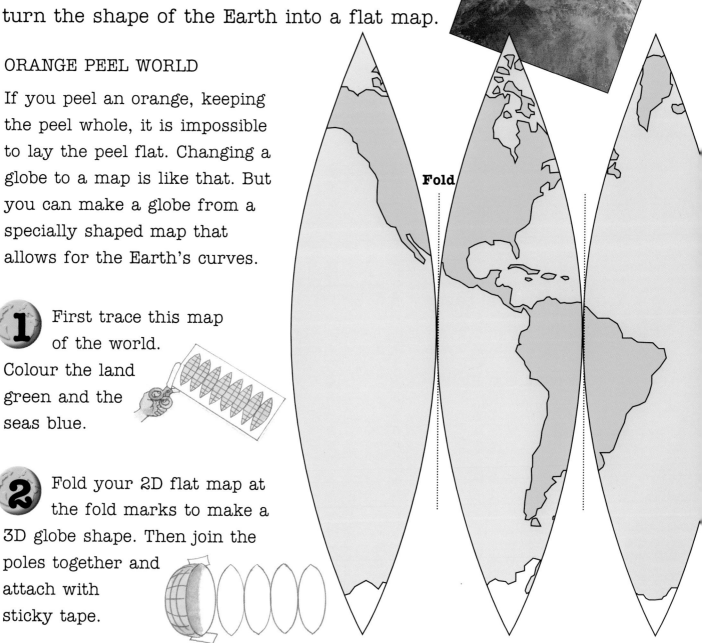

Fold

3 To suspend the globe, use sticky tape to attach a length of strong thread to the North Pole. Then watch your 3D Earth spin.

HELPFUL HINTS

● To make a stronger 3D globe, mount your flat map onto card before folding.

● To make a much bigger globe, you can enlarge your flat map on a photocopier.

● Maps of the world can look very different. Different projections produce different shapes (see page 30). Look out for maps that make the continents take on different shapes.

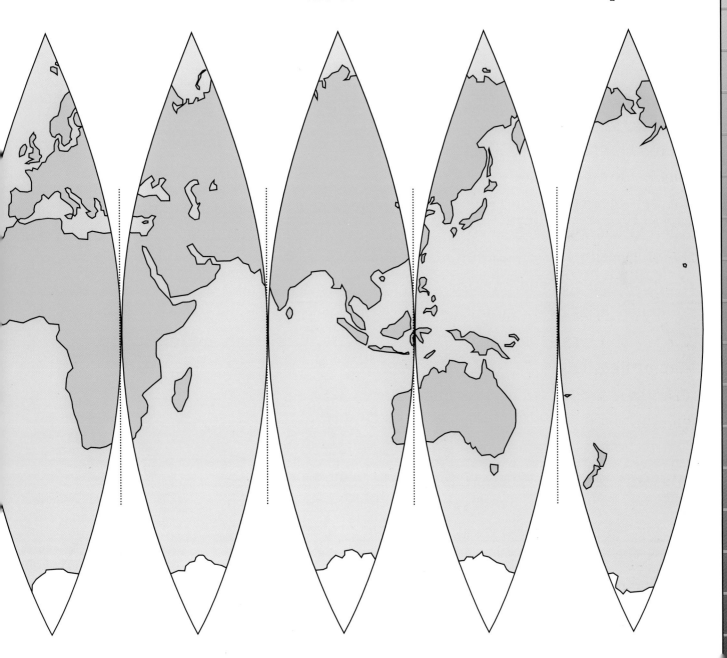

OUR WORLD

The Earth rotates (spins) around the Sun on an imaginary line called an axis, at an angle of 23.5 degrees. It is divided into halves, called hemispheres, by the Equator – another imaginary line, halfway between the North and South Pole.

North Pole

Equator

Temperate regions

Tropics

South Pole

Latitude and longitude

Imaginary horizontal lines around the Earth are called lines of latitude. They are parallel with the Equator, which is the zero degree ($0°$) line of latitude. Imaginary lines at right angles to the Equator are called lines of longitude.

Different norths

Earth is a giant magnet. Magnetic north is about 1,600 km from true north. Compass needles seek out magnetic north.

Seasons

The Earth's tilt causes the seasons. When the North Pole tilts towards the Sun, it is summer in the northern hemisphere and winter in the southern hemisphere.

Tropics and temperate regions

The tropics, on each side of the Equator, are the hottest parts of the world. Here, the Sun is overhead for most of the year. In the temperate regions, between the tropics and the poles, it is rarely extremely hot or cold.

Map projections

Imagine the globe as a glass sphere covered by a grid. A light inside casts (projects) a shadow onto paper. This is how a globe becomes a map. The shape of the paper determines the shape of the projection. Different projections distort (change the shape or size of) different features. A cylindrical projection shows the Equator the right length and makes lines of longitude seem parallel. But it doesn't show the poles, and makes Greenland look larger than South America, which is really eight times Greenland's size.

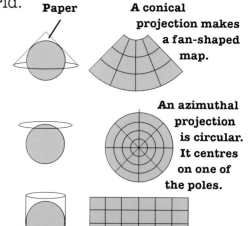

Paper

A conical projection makes a fan-shaped map.

An azimuthal projection is circular. It centres on one of the poles.

Cylindrical projection

GLOSSARY

Atlas
A book of maps.

Climate
The average weather an area has over the year.

Compass
An instrument showing the direction of magnetic north.

Earth's axis
An imaginary line through the centre of the Earth from North Pole to South Pole. The Earth rotates around its axis, which causes day and night. The tilt of the axis causes the seasons.

Equator
An imaginary line around the centre of the Earth. The zero degree ($0°$) line of latitude.

Globe
A spherical shape representing Earth.

Hachuring
Shading made up of short lines, drawn on a relief map to show the shape of the land.

Hemisphere
Half of the Earth. Summer in the northern hemisphere (north of the Equator) is winter in the southern hemisphere (south of the Equator).

Key
A list that explains the meaning of symbols used on a map or a plan.

Large-scale maps
Maps that show lots of detail but only small areas of land.

Latitude
Distance in degrees north or south of the Equator. Lines of latitude are parallel to the Equator.

Lodestone
A type of rock with magnetic properties that was used as a compass by sailors long ago.

Longitude
Distance in degrees east or west of the prime meridian, which is zero degrees ($0°$) longitude.

Map projections
Different ways to show the curved surface of the Earth as a flat map. Different projections distort the shape and size of continents and oceans in different ways.

Orienteering
Finding the way using a map and compass.

Scale
Representation of size on a map.

Small-scale maps
Maps that show little detail but large areas of land.

Symbols
Pictures or signs representing objects.

INDEX